BE YOUR OWN FR

About the Author

Ann-Marie McMahon is a graduate of University College Dublin and a registered psychologist. She is Director of Aftercare at St John of God Hospital, Stillorgan, County Dublin, where her particular interests include counselling and psychotherapy.

She has a degree in Economics together with qualifications in Public Relations and Cognitive Oriented Therapies, and has worked in these related areas, as well as in personnel management.

She conducts courses in Personal Development, Human Relations and Communications for the Sion Hill Adult Education Centre.

She has completed her Ph.D. in Human Relations at Pacific Western University, LA, USA.

Ann-Marie's first book was the best selling *Issues not Tissues: A fresh approach to personal development*, followed by *Bloom not Gloom: Self-awareness explored* and *Mixed Messages: a journey of personal discovery*. She is a contributor to the best selling *Stress File* as well as adviser to *Being You*. She is a regular contributor to newspapers, television and radio.

BE YOUR OWN FRIEND

Avoid becoming your own enemy

Ann-Marie McMahon

ASHFIELD
Press

This book was typeset by
Gough Typesetting Services for
ASHFIELD PRESS,
an imprint of Blackhall Publishing Ltd,
26 Eustace Street. Dublin 2
(e-mail: blackhall@tinet.ie)

A catalogue record for this book
is available from the British Library

ISBN 1-901658-15-5

Printed in Ireland by
Betaprint Ltd, Dublin

CONTENTS

Contents

ACKNOWLEDGEMENTS

To all those involved in publishing this book – a heartfelt thank you.

Gerry O'Connor: You have taken another risk. A special thank you to you and your team, Jackie & Tony.

Carol Devaney: Once again you have proved you are a wonderful editor. Your method of working enhances the joy of labour. Sincere thanks.

Eileen Connolly: You helped to ignite the initial flame with your superb wordprocessing skills – many thanks.

Gilbert Gough: As always your typesetting makes it all happen. Thanks again.

Mel O'Rourke: Your artistic skills has created a superb cover. Thank you and your colleague, Frank.

Rory Hafford: Thank you for your support and encouragement and your willingness to take the book on a great journey.

My readers: Thank you for your continued interest and good luck and enjoy your own lives.

INTRODUCTION

Be Your Own Friend may sound selfish, even slightly narcissistic. But, in fact, if you are not a friend to yourself, it is very difficult for others to be a friend to you.

Many of us spend our lives searching for the secret to happiness and perfect well-being when the answers are actually on our own doorstep.

If you key in the right code to your own internal system, you can question carefully and discover who you are, where you are going and where you choose to be. The answers may not always be easy, but at least they are your own.

We can tire of others telling us what to do and, at the same time, beome experts at sorting out everyone else's problems. What abour *you*?

Here is your chance to get enlightened, maybe find some solutions, discard the baggage and become a happier, more contented person. Good luck – enjoy the journey and, remember, you can get off at any stop.

Ann-Marie McMahon
March 1998

LET'S GET STARTED . . .

We all have questions, we don't all have
answers.

A good question is better than a standard
answer.

Learn to fish! Don't just catch a fish!

Within the questions sometimes lies your
own answer.

Answers can be simple, but may not be
easy.

In memory of Edel – a good friend

1 Do you feel **WORTHWHILE**?

ASK YOURSELF ...

?

How do you define yourself?

How do you feel about yourself?

How do you think about yourself?

Are you aware of your own shortcomings?

Are you happy with your own circumstances?

Do you like yourself?

Are you a constant critic of yourself?

Are you a constant critic of others?

Would you like to understand more about why you are not happy in yourself?

Would you like to make life easier for yourself?

Are you your own worst enemy?

Would you like to become more assertive, be able to cope better and become more confident?

Do you feel stuck in a rut?

Do you feel you are living on the edge?

Can you articulate what is going on?

Do you find yourself hiding from others and ultimately from yourself?

Do you believe you can change?
If not, why not?

Do you have a reasonable understanding of yourself?

Do you spend too much time thinking about yourself?

Do you try to hide the truth from yourself?

Do you ever touch base with yourself?

How much do you care about yourself?

How much do you care about others?

In what ways are you good to yourself?

In what ways are you good to others?

What are your strengths?

What are your weaknesses?

What makes you feel good or bad?

How do you show kindness to yourself?

How do you show kindness to others?

A FEW TIPS . . .

Wake up to yourself! Give yourself a chance to get to know the *real* you.

Maybe it's time to take time out and get to know who you *really* are.

Perhaps find somebody who will give you some honest feedback.

Difficult? Well then, try the professional route.

You might not like what you hear, but at least you are on the road to a better and a new you.

Listen to your own inner voice and the responses you get from other people.

Define clearly what it is you don't like about yourself and what it is you want to change.

Make a decision to change those parts of you that get in the way of making your life manageable.

Monitor your thoughts, feelings, behaviour and your ability to cope, relate and communicate.

If you want to move forward, do it now!

Remember life is not a dress rehearsal.

Create your own production in your own time, in your own environment, with your own energy and your own props.

GOOD LUCK TO THE NEW YOU AND ENJOY THE JOURNEY!

2 Do you own your **FEELINGS?**

ASK YOURSELF . . .

?

Do you ever listen to the flow of your own feelings?

Do you ever try to understand what is going on inside of you?

Do you like what you hear?

Are you aware of other peoples' feelings?

Are you spontaneous?

Do your feelings create a sense of emptiness, apathy, boredom, despair akin to a non-being?

Do your feelings interfere with your own sense of well-being?

Do feelings weigh you down?

Do feelings drain you?

Are you limited as a person in not being able to express your feelings?

Do you repress your feelings?

Do you want to feel better about yourself?

Would you like to know more about your feelings?

Do you realise that you can change the way you feel about yourself?

Do you want to know how your feelings affect your own behaviour and others?

Are you aware of how important your feelings are in defining *you* as a person?

Can you identify your own feelings?

Can you label your own feelings?

Can you identify emotional signals in others?

Can you identify emotional signals in yourself?

What language do you use to express your feelings?

What situations bring about changes in your feelings?

Would you like to shift the focus — from being repressed to being free?

A FEW TIPS ...

How are you going to achieve this?

Let's start with a 'Feelings Diary'.

Headings should include naming, labelling, identifying and knowing what experiences create certain feelings in you.

Have a checklist on when you feel good and bad about yourself.

Notice when you are in control and out of control.

Look at those feelings that upset or hurt you.

Look at underlying issues that create certain feelings.

Describe yourself in feeling terms.

Take note of the times and circumstances that create changes in your own feelings, such as:

> relationships
>
> conflict
>
> problems
>
> isolation
>
> climate
>
> criticism
>
> holidays
>
> Christmas
>
> births and deaths
>
> getting or leaving a job
>
> routine matters
>
> other life events

Try to look at the messages your feelings are sending you.

Remember feelings are your inner speech, so learn to be accurate about the messages they are sending.

Maybe it's time you tapped into deeper feelings that sometimes spoil your own happiness.

Don't be afraid of your own feelings.

Try to make friends with your feelings.

Learn to feel good *now*, not just later.

NURTURE YOUR FEELINGS — THEY WON'T AGE LIKE YOUR OUTER SELF!

3 Can you improve your **RELATIONSHIPS?**

ASK YOURSELF . . .

?

To whom do you relate on a daily basis?

Who influences your relationships with others?

Who taught you how to relate?

How did you learn to relate? From observations? From consequences?

Do you have family rules or do you have your own set of rules?

Do you have a gender script?

Do people bother you, irritate or annoy you?

Do you avoid confrontation?

Do you consider yourself shy?

Do you find it difficult to reveal yourself to others?

Could you have a better rapport with others?

Do you take responsibility for your own relationships?

Do you avoid relationships?

Do you *need* relationships even when they are causing you friction?

How many people do you relate to in any one day?

Are you in a relationship at present?

    Is it fulfilling?

    Is it fun?

    Is it enjoyable?

    Is it intimate?

    Is it painful?

    Is it serious?

What relationships are causing you the most pain?

Can you prioritise your relationships?

Can you categorise your relationships?

What role do you play in each relationship?

How do you relate to others?

How do you listen to others?

How do you react to others?

How do you talk to others?

How do you view others?

How do you think they perceive you?

A FEW TIPS ...

Give yourself a break and take time out to look at your own relationships.

You can start by getting to know yourself and relating well to yourself.

List all the relationships you have right now in your life.

Explore any barriers you create that may be obstructing your dealings with others.

Perhaps there are underlying causes, like fear or beliefs, that are very rigid or unrealistic.

Perhaps you are constantly thinking about what other people think about you and you are becoming your own worst enemy.

Perhaps your rejection of yourself is mirrored in your relationship with others.

Maybe you need to get some help in overcoming shyness, poor eye contact, inability to initiate conversations or making friendships.

Support from others, be it professional or otherwise, will help you improve your self-confidence.

Don't be afraid to risk a new relationship.

Address the areas you need to improve in significant or particular relationships.

The more you work on your own self-growth, the more you will be able to communicate and understand your vulnerabilities and strengths, and still be able to stand on your own two feet.

Try to be gentle on yourself!

Try to relate kindly to yourself.

Practise your new relating skills and behaviour.

Should you slip back into the old bad habits, don't worry! Simply pick up where you left off in your new relating programme.

Don't give up!

Your new-found confidence may prove an example to others.

REMEMBER TO BE GENTLE ON YOURSELF!

4 Are you thinking **POSITIVELY** or **NEGATIVELY?**

ASK YOURSELF . . .

?

Did you ever stop and wonder what thoughts go in and through your mind?

Do you sometimes daydream and then realise your dreams never come to fruition?

Do you sometimes lie awake at night, allowing thoughts to race around your head?

Do you ever feel weighed down by negative thinking?

Does your negative thinking spoil your feelings about yourself?

Would you like to have a 'switch off' button to control those interfering thoughts?

Do you sometimes get tired of what is going on in your head?

Do you feel like you almost have a tape in your head, with no on/off button?

Does the tape have a fast forward or playback button that you are constantly pressing?

How do you think?

Does your thinking affect your happiness?

Does your thinking affect your work performance?

Does your thinking affect your personal life?

Do you question how you think?

Do you want to change your thinking pattern?

Are you prepared to look at new possibilities?

A FEW TIPS . . .

Make a decision now to sort out your negative thinking.

Just stop NOW!

Put a pleasant thought in your head — no matter how trivial it may seem.

Observe how long you can think positive things.

Increase your positive thinking time on a daily basis, even on an hourly basis.

Watch out when you *react* and go back into auto-pilot and old habits.

Practise relaxing and feeling comfortable about yourself.

Note your 'good thinking times' in your 'Feelings Diary' (*see Chapter 2: A Few Tips*).

Take a note of what feelings come with positive thoughts.

Then watch how you behave.

If you're not getting results fast enough, don't worry!

This is not a competition.

Take all the time in the world until you feel right about yourself.

Try to enjoy your new positive outlook on life.

Don't allow any interference that may put you back on the painful road to your own negativity.

'ACCENTUATE THE POSITIVE' AND REMEMBER — ANYTHING IS POSSIBLE!

5 Are you living in **FEAR?**

?

Do you constantly live in fear?

Do you feel the fears will never go away?

Have you ever asked yourself what are you afraid of?

Did you ever wonder where your fears came from?

Do your family and friends experience the same fears?

What are you afraid of?

What are you *really* afraid of?

What is holding you back?

What situations make you afraid?

What is your worst fear?

What is a regular fear?

What is a once-off fear?

How do you suffer from your fears?

How do others suffer?

What parts of your body are affected?

What does fear prevent you from doing?

Have you ever tried to overcome your fears?

Have you tried letting go of your fears?

Why do you hold on to your fears?

What do your fears do for you?

Are you ready to let go of your fears?

Perhaps even some of them?

OK, just one of them!

What are you going to do now?

Are you comfortable with your decision?

What else might make it feel right?

A FEW TIPS ...

!

Let's look at your fears.

Look at them carefully.

Can you do something about any one of them?

When can you start?

Give it your best shot to sort out any one of your fears.

Keep a trial-and-error checklist.

Observe what works and what fails.

Stick with what helps eliminate any sense of fear.

Avoid having too high expectations.

If you fail, try again!

Try to visualise yourself without fear in your life.

Reward yourself when a fear is taken off your list.

Talk to someone if one of your fears is too difficult. Perhaps you need support.

Have a formula that can be applied to any situation in your life.

Practise! Practise! Practise!

Confront your fears and risk new feelings rather than constantly running away.

Avoid multiplying your fears or creating new ones.

Seek professional help if you are not coping sufficiently well on your own.

Have a 'fear-free hour' and monitor the positive outcome.

Extend this 'fear-free hour' to a day, to a week, to a month, to a life — *your* life!

WORK AT YOUR FEARS UNTIL THE EFFORT BECOMES EFFORTLESS

6 Do you want to **COMMUNICATE** better?

How do you communicate?

Have you ever thought about it?

Are you an active communicator?

Are you a passive person?

Do you listen to yourself?

How do you talk with others?

Have you ever looked at your words, your tone, your intonation, your interpretation?

Do you send mixed messages?

Have you hidden agendas?

Are you assertive?

Are you passive?

Are you aggressive?

Are you manipulative?

Are you sarcastic?

Do you hit out harshly and sting others with your anger?

Do you allow others to walk all over you?

Do you have a back-up system?

Do you overuse technological services, such as computers and mobile telephones?

Do you rely too much on answering machines, e-mails, faxes, voice messages — and forget to actually talk to *people*?

Do you hide behind 'techie' jargon to disguise your lack of knowledge or confidence?

Is your mode of communicating sometimes reduced to silences?

Do you avoid people rather than confront issues?

Do you criticise those who appear to communicate well?

Do you fail to listen?

Do you think the world is against you?

Can you act appropriately with your own words and actions?

Do you want to change your own communications system?

How are you going to do this?

When are you going to start?

A FEW TIPS . . .

Free yourself from irrational thinking that impedes your development.

Try to remove any deep-seated insecurities that block and threaten you from communicating positively.

Get professional help if required.

Don't feel you have to do everything on your own.

Review any relationships that are holding you back (like an aggressive partner).

Look at the choices you make in dealing with situations and people.

Ask yourself, 'Do I contribute to negative situations?'

Is the negative situation perceived or real?

Practise making assertive decisions.

Learn to live with the consequences of your own decisions.

Try to stand up for yourself.

Try to communicate what it is you *really* want.

Set limits and boundaries to protect your own vulnerability.

Understand what guidelines you are setting for yourself.

Be prepared to be flexible.

Avoid colluding.

Learn to negotiate.

Become a better listener.

Reinforce your own assertion messages.

Be realistic about demands you make on yourself and avoid too high expectations.

Be prepared to learn new methods. Treat yourself, for example, to a course in communications skills.

TRY TO BE FLEXIBLE!

7 Do you want to **CHANGE?**

ASK YOURSELF . . .

Are you stuck in a rut, bored or in need of a change?

Do you know what you want?

Are you always moaning about your life?

Do you compare yourself with others all the time?

Do you find it difficult to get out of old habits?

Do you avoid making choices?

Are you self-defeating?

Do you consider yourself weak?

Do you hide behind safe routines?

Do you see change as pointless?

Is your vocabulary sprinkled with 'I can't', 'I won't', 'I shouldn't'?

Do you cling on to your safe negative self-image?

Do you live in the hope things will change?

Do you put obstacles in the way to avoid making changes?

Are you full of uncertainties?

Do you blame others?

Do you feel it is just too much hard work?

Do you prolong a project all the time?

Does the word 'risk' terrify you?

Do you think it's a case of 'I need someone to guide me to change direction'?

Are you afraid that if you make changes, you won't like the new you or the new situation and new ideas?

Do you use your rigidity as an excuse to stay as you are?

Are you clutching on to old habits for dear life?

Do you *really* want to change?

Are you still in a rut?

Are you ruled by habits?

Do you find change difficult?

Are you afraid of change?

Is your life a mini-crisis for being so stuck?

Do you think it is too hard to find a new route?

Do you lack the courage to change?

Do you feel others can change but not you?

Do you feel you are in a tunnel, unable to move out?

How can you change?

A FEW TIPS . . .

Decide now that it is time to make some changes.

Write down what it is exactly you want to change.

Is it possible? If not, explore other options.

Set small goals and try to see these through.

Reward yourself when you achieve your goal, no matter how small.

Remember the 'three Ps' — Patience, Persist and Prioritise.

Try not to allow boredom to interfere with your moving forward.

Remember you can always go back if you feel uncomfortable or if it is too painful.

Your exploration time can be known as your 'E Plan':

    Exploration

    Experimentation

    Experiential

    Education

    Evaluation

Let your E Plan be:

    Exciting

    Exhilarating

    Emphatic — of the new you!

Learn to trust your own intuition.

Watch for those who respond to your efforts. Are they responding positively or negatively?

Sprinkle your week with little changes.

Avoid having too high expectations.

Become a good friend to yourself as part of your new changes.

Throw out excuses, crutches and blockage.

ENJOY THE NEW CHANGES!

8 What does **ANXIETY** do for you?

ASK YOURSELF ...

?

Have you ever given yourself time to look at why you are anxious?

Do you know what triggers your anxiety?

Does your anxiety interfere with your own well-being?

Does it affect others?

Would you like to do something about it?

Would you like to get rid of it? Well, some of it!

What parts of the body does it hurt?

How does it affect your thinking?

How does it affect your emotions?

Do you feel better with or without it?

Could you survive without it?

What situations create your anxiety state?

Do certain people make you anxious?

Do you sometimes want to blame
someone for your anxiety?

Does your behaviour change when you
are anxious?
>   Do you speak differently?
>   Do you think differently?
>   Do you feel differently?
>   Do you behave differently?
>   Do you look different?

Do your anxiety levels change?

Do you feel panicky sometimes? Seldom?
Often?

Do you find it difficult to make decisions?

Do you find your sleep is affected?

Are you agitated, restless or in bad humour?

Do you ever feel there is no way out of your own anxiety?

Could you possibly visualise yourself anxiety-free?

Too difficult?

Could you visualise yourself anxiety-free even for a short period?

A FEW TIPS . . .

Decide now, hard as it may seem, that you want to be free of anxiety!

Make a list of all your anxieties and why you want to be free of them.

List the exact parts of your body where anxiety affects you.

Look at how severe the pain is.

Look at times when you are less anxious and painless.

Ask yourself 'Why is this?'

Try to ascertain what helps you to be more relaxed.

Can you relax in other situations?

Look at your thinking.

Look at your feelings.

Look at your behaviour.

Look at how you cope when plagued by anxiety.

Look at your confidence levels.

Look at situations leading up to the switch from being relaxed to being anxious.

Are there any signs that indicate the switch?

Tune in to this 'switching time'.

Notice what part of your body tenses up.

Concentrate on that part and practise relaxing it.

Look at the times you can enjoy yourself.

Is there a crutch involved?

If so, try working on enjoyment *without* the crutch (whether it be alcohol, nicotine, food . . .)

Stick at what works for you and *maintain* the new relaxed you.

PICTURE YOURSELF FREE OF ANXIETY!

9 Why are you **ASHAMED?**

Do you ever find yourself saying, 'I feel so ashamed'?

Has anyone ever said to you, 'You should be ashamed of yourself!'?

Have you ever thought, 'It's such a shame'?

Do you sometimes want to bow your head in shame?

Why are you ashamed?

Who makes you feel ashamed?

Whose shame is it?

Where did this shame come from?

What does shame do for you?

Does the shame hurt?

What situations create a sense of shame for you?

Has anyone passed on shame to you?

Are you accountable to anyone for your shame?

Do you sometimes anticipate shame or shameful situations?

What feelings do you associate with your shame?

How do you behave when you are ridden with shame?

Can shame have any positive effect for you?

Do you want to rid yourself of this shame?

Is shame stopping you from moving forward?

How can you start getting rid of the shame?

A FEW TIPS ...

Take time out and give yourself a chance to look at your 'shameful' situations.

Discover on your own, or with someone else, what your shame really stems from.

Try to let go of the nasty feelings.

Seek professional help when appropriate.

Realise your own worth!

Destructive emotions only bring you down. Do everything to help bring you up!

Look at times when you are embarrassed, but not ashamed.

Realise that certain situations can make us temporarily upset, but they need not become life-long partners.

If you feel others reject you, remember you need not reject yourself.

Keep a daily diary outlining your shameful thoughts, feelings, actions.

Day by day, eliminate these shameful thoughts until there are none left.

Reward yourself for a job well done.

Visualise yourself as a person who is free of shame.

Be prepared to change direction in your life, so that you can adapt to your new shame-free lifestyle.

GOOD LUCK TO THE SHAME-FREE YOU!

10 Who makes you **GUILTY?**

ASK YOURSELF . . .

Did you ever find yourself uttering such sentiments as:

> 'She makes me so mad!'
> 'He drives me up the wall!'
> 'She drives me round the twist!'
> 'He makes me feel so guilty!'

Can anyone really make you feel guilty?

What is your guilt *really* all about?

What does your guilt do for you?

Who gives it to you?

Why do you hold on to it?

What makes you guilty?

Who makes you guilty?

Do you want to get rid of this 'feeling guilty'?

Does guilt weigh you down?

Does guilt control your life?

Does your conscience pester you?

Can you share your guilt with anyone?

Does guilt damage your health?

Does guilt play on your mind on a daily basis?

Does it affect your sleep?

Have you any techniques to assist you in ridding yourself of your guilt?

Are your guilty feelings specific?

Is your guilt associated with secrecy?

Whose voice enters your head when you are guilty?

Do you blame others for your guilt?

Is your guilt protecting you from something?

Is it difficult to examine your guilt?

Is it difficult to talk about your guilt?

If so, why?

What lies beneath the guilt?

How are you going to start ridding yourself of this 'destructive' guilt?

A FEW TIPS . . .

Get ready to throw away your guilt —
now!

Have a guilt-free day!

Difficult? Well, start with half a day.

Notice how you feel after your guilt-free
time.

Try to forgive yourself.

Try to forgive others.

Give yourself permission to be free from
the guilt that burdens you.

Develop a healthy conscience.

Talk to someone about your hidden guilt.

Examine your attitude towards yourself.

Try to discover harmony and balance within yourself, rather than remorse and recrimination.

List what it is you really feel guilty about.

Do something about it now!

Act, not react!

Look at the difference between cause and consequence in any given situation.

Does your conscience make you harsh and executionary or wise and understanding?

If you did something wrong, try and see if you can repair the damage.

If you lied, ask why?

Stop blame talk!

Try to substitute good behaviour for bad.

Avoid self-pity.

Try to change your thinking — from negative to positive.

Avoid using phrases like 'I should', 'I must', 'I have to'.

If your guilt is protecting you, find out from what.

Never give up on the search for a 'guilt-free you'.

TRAVEL LIGHT — GET RID OF THAT EXTRA BAGGAGE!

11 Can you heal those **WOUNDS?**

ASK YOURSELF . . .

?

What causes your inner wounds?

Do they hurt? A little? A lot?

Can you describe them?

Why are they there?

Who put them there?

Why are they lasting?

How do they make you feel?

Are they deep-seated and old?

Are they recent?

Are they related to specific situations?

Can you see them?

Does part of your body show external signs?

Does your physical self reveal your inner self?

Can you relate your inner wounds to outer wounds? If so, where?

Does the outer wound hide the inner one?

Do the wounds surface daily, weekly, monthly, yearly?

Do you want to keep them?

Do you want to heal them?

Do they hurt just you or you *and* others?

Can you talk about them?

Can you allow someone else to listen to your story?

Is the wound wrapped and tightened by a label?

Who gave you the label?

Is it Society's label?

What label would *you* put on it?

Is there a stigma attached?

Can you replace the label?

Are you afraid to open your wound?

Is your life consumed by your inner wounds?

Are you holding on to them for dear life?

Are you tired and worn out by them?

Are you confused by them?

Are they almost killing you?

Do you want to be rid of them?

Are you ready to let go of them?

A FEW TIPS . . .

!

Stop, look and listen to what is going on inside you!

Give up your 'victim' role and reclaim your power.

Allow yourself time to heal.

Explore gently.

Get support, professional or otherwise.

Wounds opened can also be closed.

Get a perspective on old wounds.

They may be deep-seated, but they may not be yours.

Give yourself permission to change from being passive, victimised, wounded to being active, assertive, powerful and in control.

Avoid going down the road of 'What's the use?' or 'What's the point?' or 'It's useless!'

Inner wounds can heal like outer wounds if given some TLC.*

GIVE YOURSELF SOME TENDER LOVING CARE* — AND SOME TIME!

12 What is **BLOCKING** you?

ASK YOURSELF . . .

Do you live your life with road blocks all around you, to keep the traffic of other people at bay?

Are you aware that you use barriers to ward off difficult situations?

Are they erected consciously or unconsciously?

Are they erected to deal with pent-up emotions?

Do your barriers have signs up, like:

      'Keep out — resentment at work'!

      'Keep out — jealousy at work'!

      'Keep out — perfectionist at work'!

      'Keep out — manipulation at work'!

      'Keep out — addiction at work'!

Can you identify your barriers?

How do you erect your barriers?

Do you overcompensate for your barriers?

What are the compensations? Perhaps food, alcohol, nicotine, drugs, other?

Do you try to hide your barriers?

Do you isolate yourself as a result of your barriers?

Do you own up to your barriers?

Do you want to do something about dismantling them?

Are you afraid of what might happen when you start dismantling them?

Have you some blind spots?

Are you afraid of consequences?

Do you let down your guard occasionally, only to built bigger and stronger walls later?

Are you aware of your own personal defence mechanisms?

Can you list them?

Do you waste energy justifying your defence machinery?

Do you accept the mechanisms are yours?

A FEW TIPS ...

Go on, give yourself a break! Let down that wall all around you!

You *can* take it down, brick by brick.

You don't have to do this alone. You can get support.

Choose your own support.

Focus on the experience rather than the outcome.

Acknowledge any new 'good feelings' as you tear away the bricks.

Avoid having too high expectations.

List your defence mechanisms.

Under what circumstances do you use them?

Observe how others cope without using defence mechanisms in similar circumstances.

Perhaps you can choose a different way of coping.

Allow yourself to be vulnerable!

Do it *now* — tomorrow may be too late!

Look at whether you have other agenda when using your defences.

Are you in denial of your defence mechanisms?

Are you resisting?

Are you afraid of revealing your inner self?

Try to listen to what others are really saying.

Becoming a good listener can help you understand someone else's perspective and perhaps change your own world at the same time.

Try to make sense of someone else's communications.

Check any misinterpretations.

Avoid blaming others for your defences.

RELAX! REVEAL! REJUVENATE!

13 Where is that **STRESS** coming from?

ASK YOURSELF . . .

?

Are you irritable?

Are you always in a crisis?

Are you always moaning that you have too much to do?

Do you feel too many people make too many demands on you?

Do you sometimes feel you cannot cope?

Has your workload increased?

Do you perceive a lot of tasks as difficult?

Do you avoid situations because you are too tired?

Are you tense most of the time?

Do you recognise when your body signals 'STOP!'?

Do you seek help when in pain?

Do you know what stress is?

Do you know where stress comes from?

Do you say you are suffering from stress when you know there are underlying problems you have not dealt with?

Is your environment stressful?

Is your thinking stressful?

Is your body stressed out?

Where exactly?

Are people around you stressful?

Do you react to other people's stress?

Do you get involved with others whose lives lead you into even more stress?

Are you using other substitutes to cope with your stress (such as cigarettes, alcohol, food)?

What do these substitutes do for you?

Do you want to be stress-free?

Are you abusing yourself from stress?

Are you abusing someone else due to your own stress?

Is your stress level high or low?

Do you ever take time out to assess the stresses in your life?

Would you like to take time out to examine these stresses?

When are you going to start?

A FEW TIPS ...

Let's start your DE-stress programme now!

Look at what interferes with your happiness and contentment.

List the times and places where you find yourself stressed out. Maybe situations like:

    work

    travelling

    home life

    public speaking

    negative outlook

    inability to adapt to change

List the demands made upon you through your physical being, your environment and your thought process.

Look at how you react to different situations.

Have a vision of a 'de-stressed you'.

Set about making that vision a reality.

Do it on a trial-and-error basis.

Observe how you change your thinking.

Observe how you feel about yourself.

Observe how you behave.

Observe the language you use (fade out on the 'I must', 'I should', 'I have to').

Look at your needs and decide what you can take on board and what you can throw away.

Connect with people and situations that are stress-free.

Avoid being too hard on yourself.

Forgive yourself if you make a mistake.

Get yourself fit — physically and mentally.

Have your own stress-cure recipes. Fill them up with ideas, brainwaves, notions, potions and stress-free formulae!

Have a stress-free week.

Too difficult? Try a stress-free day.

Still too difficult? What about a stress-free hour?

Learn to manage, organise and delegate.

Don't allow 'blame talk' to interfere with your stress-free diet.

Look also at your physical diet and well-being.

Remember you always have options if your diet gets boring.

Remember, too, that one day all the stress will be gone.

ENJOY LIFE — IT'S NOT A *STRESS* REHEARSAL!

14 When do you feel **THREATENED?**

ASK YOURSELF . . .

?

Do you feel uncomfortable revealing information about yourself?

Do you anticipate what others might think of you?

Are you aware of your own 'threats'?

Do you feel threatened by others?

What situations make you feel threatened?

What feelings do you associate with being threatened?

How do you cope?

How do you behave?

How do you experience threatening situations?

Do you perceive, or imagine, danger in quite ordinary situations?

What do you perceive might go wrong?

How do you protect yourself?

Do you feel threatened when others are angry?

What is this all about?

What do you do when under threat? Withdraw? Attack?

Does your body language reveal how threatened you feel?

Do you use your voice to threaten others?

If you are in a combative situation and you are threatened, do you run away, confront or engage in 'tit for tat' game-playing?

Have you ever looked at what your own threats are *really* about?

Have you ever looked at what another's threats are all about?

Do your threatening feelings lead you to further disbelief in yourself?

Are these threats to yourself interfering with your own self-regard?

Are you sometimes so threatened that you strike out with the wrong placard?

Do you find yourself threatened in relationships?

Do you use threats yourself (in the form of veiled threats) to get out of difficult situations?

Are you the victim of veiled threats?

If so, whose threats?

Do you feel you are being bullied by others?

What do these threats represent? Insults, anger, manipulation, cowardice, behaviour, criticism?

Are they flung at you out of the blue or do they creep up subtly?

Do you feel unsafe in your own home, workplace or neighbourhood?

Do you feel your space is invaded or violated?

What makes you feel unsafe?

Who makes you feel unsafe?

Why?

What is going on?

Have you done anything to make yourself, or your home, 'threatening-free'?

A FEW TIPS ...

Define the term 'threat' for yourself.

List the 'threats' you think or feel you have in your life.

Ask yourself are they real or imaginary?

Observe the threats that are yours and the threatening situations that create uncomfortable feelings.

If the threats are related to self-disclosure, take time out to look at:

> Your thinking — positive and negative?
>
> Your feelings — inadequacy, loneliness, failures, happiness?
>
> Your achievements — at work, at home?
>
> Your attitude — towards yourself, towards others?

Ask yourself why do you find it difficult to disclose yourself?

Perhaps get support to discuss this.

Look at any underlying difficulties that leave you feeling uncomfortable or threatened.

If you feel threatened by others, look at what might be going on for the other person.

Also look at when you are provoked.

If you are constantly avoiding confrontational situations, maybe you need to learn some assertion skills to cope.

If you are threatened in a real way, where you sense danger (for example, in your home), then seek help.

Look at the consequences of threatening situations (for example, mugging).

If you are threatened by criticism, anger or aggression, learn to manage these situations with coping techniques.

Get feedback from others to check how you are doing.

Don't let threatening situations get out of hand.

People who use threats to cope with situations are usually very insecure themselves.

Learn to trust your own instincts.

Avoid destructive relationships that often end up with threats and rejection.

Remember there are always several options for dealing with a threatening situation.

Remember if someone is threatening you, they may also be threatening someone else.

VALUE AND RESPECT YOUR OWN SPACE!

15 Who sets your GOALS?

?

Do you ever set goals for yourself?

Do you plan ahead?

Do you set targets?

Do you let others set goals for you?

Do you daydream?

Do you have wishes, desires and strong feelings about your future?

Do you just let things happen?

Do you long for something to happen only to end up disappointed?

Are you a drifter?

Do you ever touch base with yourself?

Do you set goals and abandon them when things don't work out your way?

Do you value yourself enough to pursue your goal?

Do you get side-tracked easily?

Are your expectations too high?

Do you just drop your goal if you fail to get past the first step?

Are you an all-or-nothing person?

Do you reward yourself when you achieve a goal?

Do you celebrate?

Do you enjoy the process involved in finding and achieving your goal?

Do you put obstacles in the way?

Do you know what you *really* want?

Have you already started?

If so, did you achieve your goal?

If not, what other options have you?

A FEW TIPS . . .

If you know what you really want, set down your goal and go for it!

Start by brainstorming ideas to achieve your goal.

Look at any obstacles and find ways to deal with them.

Look also at the possible outcome.

Remember there are always options.

Look at practical issues, such as finance, available time, other practicalities.

Perhaps do a pilot study or trial run for certain short-term goals.

Perhaps you have a problem with taking a risk, even though you really want to achieve something?

Get support — professional or otherwise.

Rehearse a situation if in doubt.

Try to lower your standards to get you going.

Achieving small, short-term goals sets you on the road to achieving greater, long-term goals.

Be prepared to have different visions if 'Vision No. 1' is definitely not a possibility.

Keep a flow chart and see how small steps fit into the larger picture.

Remember it's *your* goal!

DON'T BE AFRAID OF MAKING MISTAKES — A MISTAKE IS ONLY A MISTAKE!

16 Do you have your own **COPING** techniques?

Do you ever find yourself saying 'I don't know how to cope' or 'I just can't cope'?

Do you find yourself comparing your own inside with someone else's outside?

Do you find it difficult to cope with:
    criticism
    conflict
    confrontation
    aggression
    problem-solving

Do you feel you can solve other people's problems, but not your own?

Have you ever looked at deficits in your own personal life?

Have you explored all of your talents?

Do you have all the answers to a friend's personal relationship, but not to your own?

Do you find yourself at variance with your own coping techniques?

Are you shy?

Are you defensive?

Are you always playing games?

Are you vulnerable?

Are you over-sensitive?

Are you ill at ease socially?

Do you 'put your foot in it' all the time?

Do you avoid situations?

Do you feel stuck in a rut?

Do you feel institutionalised?

Do you feel suffocated, like being down a tunnel and don't know how to get out?

Do you feel life is about the survival of the fittest?

Do you feel as if you are sitting on a fence, watching others getting on with life?

Maybe you just don't know how?

Do you feel outside the 'social norms'?

Do you feel you just don't fit in?

Do you want to move forward, but you just don't know how?

Can you clearly identify the areas in your life where you find you cannot cope? Just to get you started, areas such as:

finance, savings, loans

study

relationships

work

illness — yourself, family

neighbours

legal problems

feelings

insecurities

conflict, problems

practical issues

loneliness

cooking

caring for a child or parent

dealing with authority figures

panic situations

having fun

communicating

surviving

Do you want to enhance those skills you have acquired recently?

A FEW TIPS ...

!

Develop your own coping strategy programme.

List the times when you cannot cope.

List the times when you can.

Specify real difficulties.

Decide now to seek help.

Get support – professional or otherwise.

Persist.

Have patience if things are not moving as fast as you would like.

Prioritise.

Work on your techniques one at a time.

Learn a new skill if necessary.

Look at alternatives.

Try to be flexible.

Use the process as part of your CSP.*

Reward yourself for your efforts.

**REMEMBER — HAVE YOUR OWN
COPING STRATEGY PROGRAMME*!**

17 Would you like to be more **CONFIDENT?**

ASK YOURSELF ...

Do you ever find that you want to hide under the covers, away from the world, because you feel you have no confidence?

Does this lack of confidence hold you back from pursuing your career, relationships, goals?

Are you shy?

Are you only shy in certain circumstances (for example, with family, neighbours, strangers, at social gatherings)?

Are you constantly comparing your own inside with someone else's outside?

Do you think everyone else is more confident than you?

Do you constantly feel an outsider because you are lacking in confidence?

Do people remind you of your shyness?

Do you use your shyness to opt out of situations?

Are you in awe of others?

Do you unintentionally attach yourself to other individuals due to your own lack of confidence?

What type of relationship is this?

Who is the dominant person?

Are you content to be always in the passive role?

Do you want to change from this role?

Do you *really* want to change?

Have you ever tried to become more confident?

Did you try, but didn't succeed?

Did you make excuses?

Does someone in your life keep putting you down and undermining any confidence you might have?

Are you tired of having low self-esteem?

Do you believe you can become more confident and have better self-esteem?

How are you going to achieve this?

A FEW TIPS ...

Now is the time for you to become a confident human being!

Use every help available, such as:

    personal development courses

    assertiveness courses

    self-awareness courses

Acknowledge your strengths.

Relax by whatever method possible.

Smile, even when you don't feel like it.

Visualise a new 'confident you'.

Realise that there are plenty of others out there feeling just like you.

Notice how your feelings change when you behave with confidence, even if you are only practising in the early stages?

Effort leads to effortless.

Compliment the new confident you with a confident environment.

Choose perhaps a new style of dressing.

Change your colours!

Throw out everything that reminds you of the dull old days.

Learn and gain knowledge.

Practise! Practise! Practise!

If there are serious underlying problems affecting your confidence, get professional help.

KEEP SMILING - THINGS *WILL* GET BETTER!

18 Who makes your **CHOICES?**

Do you ever stop and think about your life and how it is, especially for you?

Do you feel you have control over your own life?

Who chooses your behaviour?

Who chooses how you think, how you feel, how you belong?

Do you believe you have *real* choices?

Do you find it difficult to choose?

Would you prefer if someone else made decisions for you?

Are you just plain indecisive?

Who chooses your sense of well-being?

Who chooses your happiness?

Who chooses your problems, your baggage of negativity?

Who is responsible for any problems in your life and situation?

Do you have a choice to change from a problematic life to a contented life?

Do you choose sometimes to do nothing, hoping someone else will do it for you?

Do you sometimes blame others for your poor choices?

Are you stuck with your poor choices?

Does it all seem almost too difficult to comprehend?

Does it seem laborious to choose a different way of thinking?

Do different choices mean different consequences?

Does fear hold you back from choosing?

Do you feel you don't deserve new choices?

Are you in control?

Do you give away your control to someone else?

> To whom?

> How often?

Is someone else influencing and knocking your confidence to choose?

Are you tired of letting others make choices for you?

Is it easier for those around you to make choices for you?

Are you happy with the decisions made on your behalf?

If they choose incorrectly, who gets blamed?

Do you postpone making decisions?

If so, why?

Would you like to choose a different route to a new lifestyle?

A FEW TIPS . . .

Go on! Choose now and try to change your stale thinking!

Realise you *can* make a choice about how you lead your life.

Choose to end the old ways and start afresh.

Choose to end the struggle.

Choose to know you deserve the best, like anyone else.

Choose to trust yourself.

Choose to trust your own judgement.

Choose to make your own decisions and be proud of them.

Choose not to blame others for your own actions.

Choose not to be a victim.

Choose to take control.

Choose to be empowered.

Choose to reclaim power.

Choose not to limit yourself.

Choose to be flexible.

Choose to look around at what is really going on in your environment.

Choose what parts of your environment energise you.

Choose to leave the negative parts behind.

Choose to give others time and space.

Choose to be happy and enjoy life.

ENJOY YOUR CHOICES — THEY'RE YOURS!

19 Can you take **RESPONSIBILITY?**

ASK YOURSELF . . .

When did you first hear the word 'responsibility'?

Who said it?

What did it mean to you?

Were you frightened of it?

Was it something for 'grown-ups'?

Did you shy away from it?

Did you rebel against it?

Did you respond and rush headlong into taking responsibility?

Do you enjoy taking responsibility?

What are you responsible for?

To whom are you responsible?

Who is responsible for you?

Do you sometimes feel overcome by responsibility?

Do you have too much responsibility?

Are you responsible for others' actions?

Do you take on responsibilities that are not yours?

Do you enjoy being responsible?

Do you feel over-responsible?

Does too much responsibility interfere with your enjoyment of life?

Who is responsible for enjoyment in your life?

Do you associate responsibility with discipline problems, serious issues and achievements?

Who is responsible for the less serious issues?

Do you share responsibility?

Does your partner take on all the responsibility and leave you with nothing?

Do you take it all on and deprive someone else?

Do you find it difficult to delegate?

A FEW TIPS ...

Maybe it's time you looked at responsibility in your life.

Define what it means to you.

Make a list of what you are responsible for — at home, at work, in the community and family.

Have you too much or too little?

Try to delegate.

Try to let some of it go.

Try to take on more.

Try to change your outlook on certain issues.

Try to be responsible about issues that are perhaps destroying your life.

BE RESPONSIBLE FOR YOUR OWN HAPPINESS!

20 Have you your own **SUPPORT** network?

?

Do you ever feel you could do with support because you are:

   alone?

   lonely?

   ill?

   depressed?

   poor?

   outside?

   in pain?

   struggling?

   stuck in a rut?

   or

   you have huge problems?

   or

   you are suffocating in a relationship?

   or

   because you just want to talk?

Do you sometimes feel there is no support available?

Do you find it difficult to ask for support?

Are you shy about asking?

Are you embarrassed to ask?

Do you think you might lose face if you asked for support?

Do you feel you have to cope alone? Sometimes? All of the time?

Do you feel you have to put on a mask to brave the world?

Are you afraid to ask for help?

Do you wish someone would get support for you?

Do you look around at everyone else and see how they are coping, which makes you feel twice as bad?

Are you too proud to ask for help?

Do you have a nest of barriers or defence mechanisms to hide your weaknesses?

Are your barriers blocking you from
seeking help?

What are these barriers?

Do you want support?

Can you admit it to yourself?

Do you know what type of support you
want?

Can you surrender to someone helping
you?

Can you accept that others *can* help
you?

A FEW TIPS . . .

If it helps, write down the type of support you want.

Be honest with yourself now!

Perhaps there is support around you and you are refusing to avail of it?

Look at existing support networks around you, such as family, friends, relatives, colleagues, neighbours.

Become more assertive and ask for support.

Give others a chance to be your friend.

Participate in leisure pursuits and hobbies.

Test the waters. If you feel a particular person is not listening to you, try someone else. If all else fails, get professional help.

Value time and money spent on support for *yourself*.

Take time out and evaluate your health and well-being.

Take time to find creative solutions.

Take a risk and use the phone.

Avoid isolating yourself.

Become aware of self-help groups available to you.

Identify your problems.

Talk to your doctor if you have physical symptoms or are in pain.

Write it down first.

Don't bottle everything up.

Look at your 'props'.

Have a 'prop-me-up' day!

Share your props with someone else.

Look at times you are always propping others up.

Look at who props you up.

If you don't have support, go out and find it.

Look at what support you have yourself.

Your own inner resources may be greater than you think.

Put your brain in gear. Think! Think! Think!

Imagine what you want.

Talk about it.

Take action.

Turn resistance into support.

Always have reserve.

Share your reserve.

Some day you might need someone else's!

INVEST IN SUPPORT — ONE DAY IT MAY PAY DIVIDENDS!

21 How can you MOVE FORWARD?

ASK YOURSELF . . .

?

Are you your own friend?

If not, why not?

Are you, perhaps, your own enemy?

If so, why?

Do you want to be more than you are?

Do you want to have a better sense of well-being?

Do you want to be more contented?

Do you want to get out of your rut?

Do you want to get out of your tunnel?

How long have you been in the tunnel?

Do you believe in yourself?

Do you think you can change?

Do you want to change?

Are your needs being met?

Do you know what your needs are?

Are you consumed by guilt, fear, negative energy?

Is your life a struggle?

Would you like it to be different?

Do you know who is responsible for your situation?

Do you know who *you* are?

Do you know what you have?

Do you know how others perceive you?

Are you always brimming with ideas, theories, suggestions, but never put anything into practice?

Who cares for you?

Is time a problem for you?
      Too much leads to boredom?
      Too little leads to stress?

Do you have vision, drive, desire?

Are you dependent on others?

Are others dependent on you?

Do you lack energy?

Are you always tired?

Do you sleep every night? Some nights? Seldom?

Is finance a problem?

Can you imagine life better than what it is now?

Do you project all the time and forget about the process?

Is there a road you wish to travel, but you feel you're always in a cul de sac?

Do you constantly compare your own inside with someone else's outside?

Are you obsessed with labels, such as 'victim'?

Do you see relationships as just complex, complicated connections?

Do you hide yourself away from human contact?

Are you careless about looking after yourself?

Are you a constant critic — of yourself and others?

Are you wrapped up in 'poor me' coatings?

Are you caught up in your 'sell-by date'?

Are you worn out from too much negative living?

Are you always blaming others?

Are you consumed by unhealthy baggage?

Is it time you did something to move forward?

How can you do this?

A FEW TIPS ...

!

Start *now*!

Think *now*!

Experience *now*!

Decide *now* to change things you don't like about yourself and your situation.

Make a list of what you don't like about your life.

Check it! Maybe it's not all that bad.

Pace yourself and decide to change things slowly.

Prioritise — decide what is most important.

Have patience!

Think of options.

Persist!

Be flexible in your change programme.

Get support.

Make time.

Decide what you want to be.

Decide what you want to have.

Decide where you want to go.

Decide what is important.

Decide who is important.

Decide who affects you.

Decide who bothers you.

Decide who is good to you.

Be kind to yourself!

Look at your physical health.

Look at your emotions.

Look at your mental state.

Look at your needs.

Look at any deficit in your skills.

Decide to learn a new skill.

Become mentally and physically fit.

Practise! Practise! Practise!

Persist! Persist! Persist!

Prioritise! Prioritise! Prioritise!

Give yourself permission to make mistakes.

A mistake is only a mistake.

Go from 'out of control' to 'in control'.

Don't give away your control.

Eliminate any additional addictive substances one by one.

Eliminate any obsessions, labels or strange behaviour that may be interfering with your life.

Do it slowly, daily and get support if necessary.

Focus on your strengths.

Don't be afraid of your own vulnerabilities.

Don't be afraid of others' vulnerabilities.

Try something new.

Risk new feelings.

Feelings are just that — feelings. You can always change them.

Have compassion for yourself and others.

Balance your life.

Emphasize your positive side.

Have a daily 'thank-you' list.

BECOME A TRULY GOOD FRIEND TO YOURSELF!

P. S. You might become friends to many more!

For your own **PERSONAL RECORD**

Do you feel WORTHWHILE?

Do you own your FEELINGS?

Can you improve your RELATIONSHIPS?

Are you thinking POSITIVELY or NEGATIVELY?

Are you living in FEAR?

Do you want to COMMUNICATE better?

Do you want to CHANGE?

What does ANXIETY do for you?

Why are you ASHAMED?

Who makes you GUILTY?

Can you heal those WOUNDS?

What is BLOCKING you?

Where is that STRESS coming from?

When do you feel THREATENED?

Who sets your GOALS?

Do you have your own COPING techniques?

Would you like to be more CONFIDENT?

Who makes your CHOICES?

Can you take RESPONSIBILITY?

Have you your own SUPPORT network?

**PREVIOUSLY PUBLISHED BY
ANN-MARIE MCMAHON**

Issues not Tissues

The author introduces a new down to
earth approach to personal
development. The fresh ideas offered in
this book cover problems many of us
experience in our daily lives. Whether
dealing with troublesome relationships,
lack of self-confidence, addiction or the
blues, we are urged to deal with the
issues involved rather than reach for the
tissue box.

Issues not Tissues takes an innovative
and imaginative look at all aspects of life
and provides practical advice on how to
rejuvenate and re-evalue out mental and
emotional state. Ms McMahon reminds us
that there are always options available,
and shares some useful techniques for
assessing which ones are most helpful.

Issues not Tissues is vital for everyone
who thinks they're perfect and for those of
us who know we're not|

ISBN 1-871305-11-X   £5.99

Bloom not Gloom!

Have you ever felt 'stuck in a rut', 'cheesed off' or 'all alone'? Have you ever 'put your foot in it', or felt consumed by anxiety, fear or indecision?

  If you can honestly answer 'yes' to any of these questions, then read on!

  The author tries to answer these questions and show the way forward in her new book *Bloom not Gloom!*

  Bloom not Gloom! helps to explore you inner self and find a route for you to blossom into the NEW YOU. So throw out all that negative, gloomy old baggage you haul around every day and start to really live!

ISBN 1-873848-01-9   £6.99

Mixed Messages

The valley of squinting windows, the ceol agus craic culture, the nod and wink society – sure it could happen to a bishop – bury your head in shame – Irish cliches or confusing messages!

What do these statements really mean? Who are they focussed at? *Mixed Messages* attempts to unravel the 'mixed messages' that are hurled at us on a daily basis.

They come in the guise of innuendos, put downs, side kicks, threats, misguided opinions, remarks, criticisms, silences and designer gossip, leaving us very shackled by hurt, pain, shame, labels, stigmas, guilt, secrets, scars and inner wounds.

The author gives us an insight into what might be behind those veiled threats and help alleviate our blurred vision.

Mixed Messages is a must for all.

ISBN 1-901658-00-7   £7.99